THE CHINESE HOROSCOPES LIBRARY

Ox

KWOK MAN-HO

DK

A DORLING KINDERSLEY BOOK

Senior Editor	Sharon Lucas
Art Editor	Camilla Fox
Managing Editor	Krystyna Mayer
Managing Art Editor	Derek Coombes
DTP Designer	Doug Miller
Production Controller	Antony Heller
US Editor	Laaren Brown

Artworks: Danuta Mayer 4, 8, 11, 17, 27, 29, 31, 33, 35;
Giuliano Fornari 21; Studio Illibill 25; Jane Thomson; Sarah Ponder.

Special Photography by Steve Gorton. Thank you to The British Museum, Chinese Post
Office, Percival David Foundation of Chinese Art, and The Powell-Cotton Museum.

Additional Photography: Eric Crichton, Jo Foord, Steve Gorton, Dave King, David Murray,
Stephen Oliver, Tim Ridley, Clive Streeter, Matthew Ward.

Picture Credits: Bridgeman Art Library/Oriental Museum, Durham University 12; Courtesy
of The Board of Trustees of the Victoria & Albert Museum 15.

First American Edition, 1994
4 6 8 10 9 7 5

Published in the United States by DK Publishing, Inc., 95 Madison Avenue,
New York, New York 10016

Copyright © 1994
Dorling Kindersley Limited, London
Text copyright © 1994 ICOREC

Visit us on the World Wide Web at
http://www.dk.com

ISBN 1-56458-600-6
Library of Congress Catalog Number 93-48006

Reproduced by GRB Editrice, Verona, Italy
Printed and bound in Hong Kong by Imago

CONTENTS

INTRODUCING CHINESE HOROSCOPES

For thousands of years, the Chinese have used their astrology and religion to establish a harmony between people and the world around them.

The exact origins of the twelve animals of Chinese astrology – the Rat, Ox, Tiger, Rabbit, Dragon, Snake, Horse, Ram, Monkey, Rooster, Dog, and Pig – remain a mystery. Nevertheless, these animals are important in Chinese astrology. They are much more than general signposts to the year and to the possible good or bad times ahead for us all. The twelve animals of Chinese astrology are considered to be a reflection of the Universe itself.

YIN AND YANG

The many differences in our natures, moods, health, and fortunes reflect the wider changes within the Universe. The Chinese believe that

every single thing in the Universe is held in balance by the dynamic, cosmic forces of yin and yang. Yin is feminine, watery, and cool; the force of the Moon and the rain. Yang is masculine, solid, and hot; the force of the Sun and the Earth. According to ancient Chinese belief, the concentrated essences of yin and yang became the four seasons, and the scattered essences of yin and yang became the myriad creatures that are found on Earth.

YIN AND YANG SYMBOL
White represents the female force of yin, and black represents the masculine force of yang.

The twelve animals of Chinese astrology are all associated with either yin or yang. The forces of yin rise as Winter approaches. These forces decline with the warmth of Spring, when yang begins to assert

itself. Even in the course of a normal day, yin and yang are at work, constantly changing and balancing. These forces also naturally rise and fall within us all.

Everyone has their own internal balance of yin and yang. This affects our tempers, ambitions, and health. We also respond to the changes of weather, to the environment, and to the people who surround us.

THE FIVE ELEMENTS

All that we can touch, taste, or see is divided into five basic types or elements – wood, fire, earth, gold, and water. Everything in the Universe can be linked to one of these elements.

For example, the element earth is linked to four animals – the Ox, Dragon, Ram, and Dog. This element is also linked to the color yellow, sweet-tasting food, and the

emotion of desire. The activity of these various elements indicates the fortune that may befall us.

AN INDIVIDUAL DISCOVERY

Chinese astrology can help you balance your yin and yang. It can also tell you which element you are, and the colors, tastes, parts of the body, or emotions that are linked to your particular sign. Your fortune can be prophesied according to the year, month, day, and hour in which you were born. You can identify the type of people to whom you are attracted, and the career that will suit your character. You can understand your changes of mood, your reactions to other places and to other people. In essence, you can start to discover what makes you an individual.

DIVINATION STICKS
Another ancient and popular method of Chinese fortune-telling is using special divination sticks to obtain a specific reading from prediction books.

CASTING YOUR HOROSCOPE

The Chinese calendar is based on the movement of the Moon, unlike the calendar used in the Western world, which is based on the movement of the Sun.

Before you begin to cast your Chinese horoscope, check your year of birth on the chart on pages 44 to 45. Check particularly carefully if you were born in the early months of the year. The Chinese year does not usually begin until January or February, and you might belong to the previous Chinese year. For example, if you were born in 1961 you might assume that you were born in the Year of the Ox. However, if your birthday falls before February 15 you belong to the previous Chinese year, which is the Year of the Rat.

THE SIXTY-YEAR CYCLE
The Chinese measure the passing of time by cycles of sixty years. The twelve astrological animals appear five times during the sixty-year cycle, and they appear in a slightly different form every time. For example, if you were born in 1949

you are an Ox Inside the Gate, but if you were born in 1961, you are an Ox on the Way.

MONTHS, DAYS, AND HOURS
The twelve lunar months of the Chinese calendar do not correspond exactly with the twelve Western calendar months. This is because Chinese months are lunar, whereas Western months are solar. Chinese months are normally twenty-nine to thirty days long, and every three to four years an extra month is added to keep approximately in step with the Western year.

One Chinese hour is equal to two Western hours, and the twelve Chinese hours correspond to the twelve animal signs.

The year, month, day, and hour of birth are the keys to Chinese astrology. Once you know them, you can start to unlock your personal Chinese horoscope.

	Water
	Earth
	Gold
	Wood
	Yin
	Fire
	Yang

CHINESE ASTROLOGICAL WHEEL

In the center of the wheel is the yin and yang symbol. It is surrounded by the Chinese astrological character linked to each animal. The band of color indicates your element, and the outer ring reveals whether you are yin or yang.

· OX ·
MYTHS AND LEGENDS

The Jade Emperor, heaven's ruler, asked to see the Earth's twelve most interesting animals. When they arrived, he was impressed by the Ox's reliability, and awarded it second place.

The Ox is a highly respected creature, because it plows the land and helps with the harvest. Many Chinese do not eat beef, considering it unjust to kill the creature that deserves thanks. The Ox is a symbol of Spring, the time of the ceremonial plowing. It is also linked to water, and bronze or stone figures of oxen were often thrown into rivers in the belief that they would stop the riverbanks from bursting.

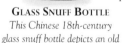

GLASS SNUFF BOTTLE
This Chinese 18th-century glass snuff bottle depicts an old man astride an ox.

FARMER CHIN AND THE OX

Long ago, Farmer Chin had a very small field of hard soil in which nothing had grown for years. He bought an ox, a big, gentle

creature. Seeing the poverty of Farmer Chin's family, the good, kind ox was determined to do all he could to help. The ox and the farmer worked from dawn to dusk. The ox's power and strength broke the soil, and his manure was used as fertilizer for the young plants. Fifteen years later, the farmer was wealthy and had a large house full of servants. But the old ox still lived in his little pen, ate poor food, and had to work very hard. One day, the ox broke a leg. "What use is that ox to me?" said Farmer Chin, and ordered that it be slaughtered. An old man suddenly approached and said, "This ox has helped you make your fortune. Can't you now allow him to rest?" Farmer Chin ignored the old man. As the ox's throat was cut, Farmer Chin felt a terrible pain in his neck. He fell immediately to the ground, dead, and the ox and the old man disappeared.

The farmer's soul was grasped and dragged into a courtroom. It contained the old man, who was King Ch'in-kuang, ruler of the first hell. Beside him stood the old ox, now transformed into an official of the court of hell.

The ox took Farmer Chin to a mirror. "Look within," boomed the king. "See all the creatures whose lives you have taken for food or sport." All the animals and birds the farmer had ever eaten or killed appeared in the mirror, including the old ox. The king ordered that Farmer Chin be thrown into the most terrible pit for his lack of compassion for all creatures, but most especially, for the kind ox.

Chinese legend still says that the first official to be seen after death is the ox-headed god of the first hell.

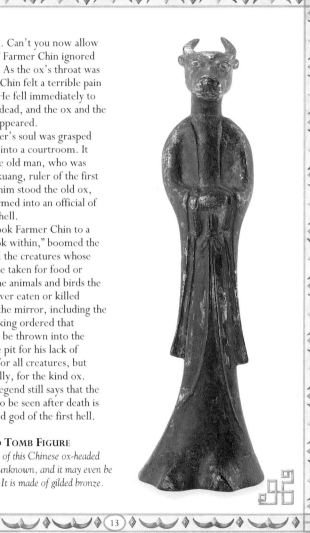

OX-HEADED TOMB FIGURE
The exact date of this Chinese ox-headed tomb figure is unknown, and it may even be fairly modern. It is made of gilded bronze.

· OX ·
PERSONALITY

Honest, placid, and always considerate, the Ox never acts on mere whim. It refuses to be influenced by gossip or trivia, and ponders all the angles of every situation.

Once you have completed a thorough assessment of any situation, you carry your course of action through to the appropriate end. You need plenty of time to build up your considerable reserves of strength. Although you may be slow to start, by the time others are exhausted or confused, you can still be found in steady pursuit of your goal.

MEDALLION BOWL
This Ch'ing dynasty yellow-ground medallion bowl depicts the Ox in a late winter scene.

MOTIVATION
You are very sure of your own mind and will not be swayed. If your interest is not aroused, no amount of temptation and persuasion will make you respond or react. You are solidly reliable, and always mean and do

what you say. You have a strong streak of stubbornness and a tendency to be outspoken. These traits make you resistant to advice, and you can be intolerant and scathing toward people who do not share your great persistence.

THE INNER OX
Essentially, you are stable and well balanced, and your steadiness is a genuine inspiration to other people. However, if you are provoked, or if your patience is pushed to its limits, your temper is furious and unrelenting.

At these times it is best for you to be left alone, since you can only calm down of your own accord. You are

CLOISONNE OX
Sturdy and upright,
this Chinese ox-shaped
vessel suggests the strength,
stature, and stubbornness of the
Ox personality. It is cloisonné
enamel on copper with gilding,
and dates from the Ch'ing
dynasty (1749–1795).

an independent character and are never easily impressed by the fashionable. You are much more comfortable and secure with the traditional and the familiar.

You dislike any form of change, particularly if it is forced upon you. However, you are invariably able to cope with most situations.

If you do have any doubts about yourself and the direction in which you are heading, you much prefer to keep your own counsel.

You are a faithful and trustworthy friend and will always be helpful in times of need.

In emotional affairs, you are not particularly passionate or romantic, but you are faithful and caring.

THE OX CHILD

The young Ox is serious and practical, but may be too dedicated to its schoolwork. It needs every encouragement to relax, have fun, and enjoy itself.

· OX ·
LOVE

Steadiness, reliability, and sincerity are much more important to the Ox than tumultuous emotion, searing passion, or the trappings of romance.

Once you have found your partner, you are likely to be thoroughly devoted and loving. You need to be absolutely sure of your own mind before you commit yourself to anyone, but once you have made a commitment, you remain sincere. Your partner should never make the mistake of taking advantage of you, for once you have been deceived, you are unlikely ever to forgive or forget.

You may neglect romantic anniversaries, but you will always be available when your loved one needs support. Occasionally, a stubborn streak may rise to the surface, but nevertheless, you try not to be hurtful.

Ideally, you are suited to the Rooster or the Snake. The sociable Rooster acts as a complement to your steady nature, and you are equally reasonable and reliable. The Snake will feel safe and secure in your presence and will happily allow you to arrange its home life.

You should find the Rat's intelligence and sincerity highly attractive, and the Rat will enjoy

GODDESS OF LOVE
Kuan Yin is a powerful figure in Chinese mythology. Once a male Buddhist deity, she is now known as the goddess of mercy, and as Sung-tzu, the giver of children.

CHINESE COMPATIBILITY WHEEL

Find your animal sign, then look for the animals that share its background color – the Ox has a yellow background and is most compatible with the Snake and the Rooster. The symbol in the center of the wheel represents double happiness.

your earnestness. The mischievous Monkey is a particularly good match for you – it appreciates your honesty and will gently tease you when you become too serious. Your steady nature appeals to the Rabbit, who always needs to feel harmonious and secure. The Pig will welcome your fondness for peace and quiet, although it is likely to find your innate good sense rather frustrating at times.

ORCHID

In China, the orchid, or Lan Hua, is an emblem of love and beauty. It is also a fertility symbol and represents many offspring.

Unfortunately, your romantic forecast is not quite so healthy when considering emotional relationships with the Ram, Horse, Dragon, or Dog. This is mainly because the Ram thinks and acts too quickly, the Horse is too lively and passionate, and the Dragon and the Dog are too willful and imaginative.

The Tiger is also unlikely to be a very good partner for you – its sheer unpredictability will disturb you, and your conscientiousness will not suit the Tiger's wandering spirit.

· OX ·
CAREER

The Ox is a thorough and efficient worker. It does not take kindly to interruption or interference, but will gladly take on the burden of responsibility.

Wheat

FARMER
Harvesting crops, collecting dairy produce, and working on the land are satisfying pursuits for the extremely hardworking Ox.

Dairy produce

Chinese rouge box

OX ON A BOX
This rouge box is from 17th- or early 18th-century China. The Chinese consider the Ox to be a beast of burden, and here it is depicted carrying an old man, probably Lao Tzu, the legendary founder of Taoism.

Chinese musical instrument

BUILDING MANAGER

The position of building manager requires fine attention to detail and a willingness to take responsibility. The Ox possesses both of these qualities and has the added bonus of a steady, reliable personality. The natural attribute of thinking carefully before making important decisions is useful to a building manager.

Building manager's keys

Oven mitt

TEACHER

The Ox makes an excellent teacher, for it relishes a busy and well-organized schedule. Perhaps a teacher taught a pupil to play this bronze musical instrument in China in the 1st century BC.

WORKER WITH FOOD

In China, the Ox is known as the beast that draws the plow. As a result, the Ox is very well suited to working with agricultural products.

Soldier's boots

ARMED FORCES

If the Ox decides to join the armed forces, it is likely to be extremely successful. It is single-minded and will not regret its decision.

· OX ·
HEALTH

*Yin and yang are in a continual state of flux within the
body. Good health is dependent upon the balance of yin
and yang being constantly harmonious.*

There is a natural minimum and maximum level of yin and yang in the human body. The body's energy is known as ch'i and is a yang force. The movement of ch'i in the human body is complemented by the movement of blood, which is a yin force. The very slightest displacement of the balance of yin or yang in the human body can quickly lead to poor health and sickness.

LINGCHIH FUNGUS

*The fungus shown in this detail
from a Ch'ing dynasty bowl is
the "immortal" lingchih fungus,
which symbolizes longevity.*

GINGER ROOT

*In Chinese medicine, ginger
root is usually
prescribed for its
abundant yang, or
warming, qualities.*

However, yang illness can be cured by yin treatment, and yin illness can be cured by yang treatment. Everybody has their own individual balance of yin and yang. It is likely that a hot-tempered person will have strong yang forces, and that a peaceful person will have strong yin forces. Your nature is closely identified with your health, and before Chinese medicine can be prescribed, your moods must be taken into account. A balance of joy, anger, sadness, happiness, worry, pensiveness, and fear must always be maintained. This fine balance is known in China as the Harmony of the Seven Sentiments.

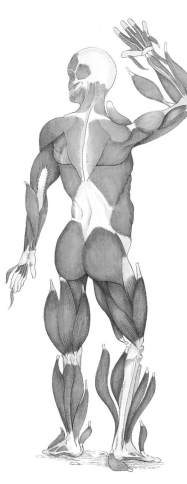

Born in the Year of the Ox, you are associated with the element earth. This element is linked with the spleen, pancreas, stomach, muscles, and mouth. These are the parts of the human body that are most relevant to the pattern of your health. You are also associated with the emotion of desire and with sweet-tasting food.

Ginger root (*Zingiber officinale*) is associated with your Chinese astrological sign. It is used for its yang, or warming qualities, which can combat symptoms of nausea, dissipate mucus, and stimulate the stomach and the intestines.

Ginger root can be prescribed as treatment for colds, or for any ailments that involve coughing. Preserved ginger root is often used to alleviate motion sickness.

Chinese medicine is highly specific; therefore, never take ginger root or any other natural medicine unless you are following professional advice from a fully qualified Chinese or Western doctor.

ASTROLOGY AND ANATOMY

Your element, earth, is associated with the digestive system. The stomach is a yang organ, and the pancreas, found behind the stomach, is a yin organ.

· OX ·
LEISURE

The Ox has a placid but determined nature. It has excellent reserves of physical energy, and once it has taken up a new activity, it pursues it wholeheartedly.

BOXING AND WRESTLING
The Ox is immensely strong and energetic, but it is not particularly aggressive. Boxing and wrestling are ideal sports for the Ox, because they allow it to use its strength and expend its energy in a skillful way and in a controlled environment.

Boxing gloves

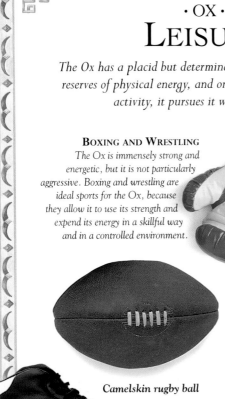

Camelskin rugby ball

High-sided rugby boot

RUGBY
Playing rugby has great appeal for the Ox – it is a traditional sport, and the Ox is rarely interested in or impressed by the latest fads or fashions. Rugby was first played in 1823 at Rugby school in England, hence the sport's name. It is also a very physical sport, in which the Ox can use its strength and endurance while enjoying being outdoors among the elements.

WINING AND DINING

Hospitality is one of the Ox's best qualities. It is happiest in the company of old friends, and is most comfortable in a familiar environment. Consequently, it loves to wine and dine at home, and will make every effort to ensure the comfort of its guests.

Glasses of wine and red rose

OX VASE

This purple and turquoise ox was used as a vase in Ch'ing dynasty China (1662–1722).

Ski

Ski wear and gloves

Porcelain ox

SKIING

The Ox finds skiing exhilarating because it is a very physical outdoor sport. The Ox also enjoys being outside in a harsh, cold environment, and likes to keep its strong, powerful body under firm control – skiing allows it to do so.

· OX ·
SYMBOLISM

In Chinese astrology, each of the twelve animals is linked with a certain food, direction, color, emotion, association, and symbol.

Chinese ox

COLOR
In China, fertile earth has a yellow hue. Yellow was the imperial color, worn by the emperor as the First Son of the Earth. The color yellow is also linked with the Ox. This yellow gold, glazed model of an ox is from China's Ch'ing dynasty.

FOOD
There are five tastes according to Chinese astrology – salty, acrid, bitter, sweet, and sour. Sweet foods, such as cashews, are associated with the Ox.

Cashews

Antique Chinese compass

Section of a map of Rome

DIRECTION

The Chinese compass points south, whereas the Western compass points north. The Chinese compass has an extra direction, the center, which is the Ox's direction.

ASSOCIATION

The capital city and its life are linked with the Ox.

SYMBOL

The Ox's symbol is the plumb line, which is used to measure the depth of water.

Plumb line

EMOTION

Desire is the emotion that is connected with the Ox.

Baby expressing desire

OX IN THE SEA

~ 1925 1985 ~

According to Chinese legend, the Ox led the race to cross the waters and be the first animal in the Chinese calendar, but was robbed of victory by the Rat.

Water is a safe and comfortable environment for any Ox, and the Ox in the Sea is particularly strong and tenacious. It is likely that you have always lived happily and confidently in your environment.

CHILDHOOD
When you were a child, there were probably many people to care for you, such as your parents, other relatives, and friends. Their love and encouragement gave you an extremely positive start in life.

PERSONALITY
You are linked to a seedling leaving the seed and reaching toward the light. In the same way that the seedling blossoms when it eventually reaches the light, so you have been guided throughout your life to realize your full potential. You are also associated with spring, a time

renowned for growth and new life. This means that you are blessed by powerful forces.

You are an excellent learner and are willing to tackle anything new, even though this goes against the grain of the usually reticent Ox.

FEMALE CHARACTERISTICS
The female Ox in the Sea is highly talented, but may sometimes need to watch her temper. She is invariably self-assured, but could be more patient with those who do not share her sense of security.

RELATIONSHIPS
Oxen in the Sea should find little difficulty in attracting other people and will usually have happy and successful emotional relationships. However, you have a desire to travel and enjoy the stimulus of new places, faces, and challenges.

Ox in the Sea

PARENTHOOD

It should be possible for you to develop an extremely rewarding relationship with your children, which will hold great importance for you. This link is worth nurturing, particularly as your own relationship with your parents could prove unsatisfactory over the years.

As you grow older and become more confident, it is likely that you will simply have to be independent and go your own way in life.

Your family may sometimes find this difficult to understand, but you should be able to dispel any tension by always being willing to rebuild the bridges between you.

OX IN THE LAKE

~ 1937 1997 ~

In China, water buffalo calmly stand their ground in the rice fields, robust and unswerving. The Ox in the Lake is equally sturdy and self-confident in any environment.

You are associated with a nail, which symbolizes steadfastness and solidity. The nail is the pivot, and it also holds all things together. You are invariably extremely stable throughout your life – you stand firm while everything swirls around you like the waters of a lake.

PERSONALITY

You are secure, calm, and kind. Because you are perceived to be dependable, many people should feel that they can confide in you.

All Oxen in the Lake are competent and skilled, but the female in particular is noted for her abilities and for the way in which she uses her talents to the utmost.

CAREER

Your career is highly likely to be prosperous because you are a person of your word and can always be depended upon when times become difficult. As long as you remain true to your calling, your reliability is likely to bring you happiness and financial security.

However, do not expect wealth to come too quickly, and remember that it is highly unlikely to be made overnight at someone else's expense. Instead, your fortune will be accrued gradually, as a result of years of hard, honest work, and as people learn to trust you.

RELATIONSHIPS

If you are careful in your choice of partner, you can have a good relationship. Since you are so dependable, you have the ability to help the flighty to settle and can also act as a rock for the weak.

You must always beware of unscrupulous characters such as the Rat, however, who will attempt to

Ox in the Lake

prey upon your charity, rely upon your strength, and use you for their own ends. Try not to allow yourself to be exploited.

Because you never rush into things, you are likely to have children in your later years. This will probably be for the best, because you will have become more capable of supplying your children with the necessary love, support, and care.

PROSPECTS

Do not expect too much of your youth, since it is during these early years that you will develop your strengths. Instead, try to look forward to your middle years, when you are much more likely to reap what you have sown.

The trust people have placed in you over the years should be rewarded, and you will have become known as a trustworthy person. People will increasingly turn to you for guidance, and as a result, your own career and fortune are likely to blossom. If you remain true to yourself, you should end your days respected and at peace.

OX INSIDE THE GATE

~ 1949 2009 ~

The Ox Inside the Gate tends to be an impatient creature. It wants to enjoy its freedom, and consequently finds any restriction to be extremely unpleasant.

You are linked to the warp and the weft of thread that is woven into cloth. This signifies that you are meant to be part of a larger whole, but there is likely to be part of you that wants to break free.

PERSONALITY

Your impatience and curtness are often likely to make you speak your mind openly. Try to take care that your love of forthright speaking and of telling the plain truth are not unnecessarily cutting and hurtful to other people.

Although your abruptness is usually admirable if you know how to use such insight wisely, it can be damaging and painful if used indiscriminately.

It will do you no harm to remember that although you are an Ox Inside the Gate and wish to push it aside carelessly and rush off to enjoy your liberty, nevertheless a significant part of you is also called to be part of the weft and warp of a much greater pattern.

All Oxen are likely to be strong and dependable, and you will always find yourself in demand. This can be unsettling for you, because you have a tendency to go against the grain. Try to control the rebellious habit of going off and doing what you want. It is likely that money will always restrain you, anyway. Do not fight against this – instead try to see it as a useful constraint.

FEMALE CHARACTERISTICS

Because of the influence of the yin force, the female Ox Inside the Gate is renowned for being clever and for involving herself in all kinds of issues. She invariably resents the barriers that restrain her and will gladly lead the fight for equal rights.

Ox Inside the Gate

However, she may have to watch this confrontational tendency and should discern between the barriers that matter and those that do not.

RELATIONSHIPS

Anyone born in these years is likely to be very attractive, both physically and mentally. Consequently, you may find yourself the center of considerable attention. Combined with your wish to break free from anything that restricts you, this could mean that you will have more than one committed relationship.

Sometimes your committed relationship may seem like the Gate that restricts you. Make sure that it is absolutely necessary for you to break free, and carefully consider whether you can remain woven into the fabric of this relationship. Try not to act hastily, but do not be too surprised when you do, for it is in your nature to behave in this way.

By the time you reach your late middle age, you should feel more content, and your career and personal relationships are likely to blossom around this time.

OX ON THE WAY

~ 1901 1961 ~

Your own way in life can sometimes seem unclear, but your Ox perseverance and strength should help you to meet the challenges that you will invariably face.

You are highly sociable, enjoyable company and have a friendly nature. Others think highly of you, and you are always willing to put yourself out for them. You have good, rewarding friendships, too. A certain sadness is linked with you, however, and if it is not handled correctly, it can soon turn to bitterness.

YOUTH

When you were in your youth, it is likely that something frightening happened to you. It could have been an accident, a disappointment, an unpleasant experience, or even an upsetting failure at something that you considered important. Whatever it may have been, you run the risk of being knocked off course for life.

You need to learn to live with whatever has happened in your past. Try not to allow it to make you cynical or resentful, for this could

spoil your basically good nature. Once you have explored these negative feelings and have them under control, you should find that your life is very much easier to live and to enjoy.

FEMALE CHARACTERISTICS

The female Ox on the Way should never despair, for she has a very good chance of leading a happy and comfortable life. As long as she learns to cope with any early disappointments in a positive way, and if she is blessed with a little luck, she should easily fulfill her potential.

CAREER

The professional life of any Ox on the Way is unlikely to be overly problematic, and your skills should be in high demand. Unfortunately, this does not necessarily mean that you will be wealthy.

Ox on the Way

As with all Oxen, wealth will only come to you through hard work and over a long period of time. Do not rush, nor expect too much too soon. Because you are associated with the Autumn, you should find prosperity and peace in your later years.

RELATIONSHIPS

Any Ox born in these years is likely to have happy relationships and a good family life, but could also experience some difficult times.

Problems of an emotional nature can be avoided if you try not to make hasty decisions concerning your family, and if you do not expect too much help from them. Look instead to your considerable inner strengths and to the many good friends who truly appreciate you.

PROSPECTS

The passing of time and a little patience should ensure that you end your days in a happy and contented state. By taking careful stock of yourself, you can reasonably expect a long, fulfilled life. But do not be in a hurry – wealth and security are likely to be a gift of time and of your own strength of resolve.

Ox Outside the Gate

~ 1913 1973 ~

This is an immensely powerful Ox. For the Ox Outside the Gate, the innate strength of the Ox is combined with the blessing brought about by correct behavior.

Yov are associated with Winter. This is a symbol of old age and death, but the Ox Outside the Gate is also associated with happy, auspicious days. This means that if you always do the right thing, you will enjoy good fortune, and even the dead days of winter should be enlivened.

You are linked with a grass mat, on which offerings to the dead were placed. This symbolism is highly propitious, for any offerings made to the dead should ensure that the living gain great benefit and merit.

Personality

You tend to want to do things properly and are usually rewarded. You should have a successful life, and earn great respect, but do not be surprised if it takes some time before you achieve your rewards. Try not to lose heart when things do not go your way immediately.

Female Characteristics

The female Ox Outside the Gate has a tendency to be unthinking in her actions. She invariably finds it easier to be offhand when she should be polite and to be cutting in her remarks when it might be wiser to restrain herself.

She is well advised to attempt to balance her wit and intellect with politeness and respect for others, and should always be prepared to apologize quickly for any unruly or unreasonable behavior.

Career

Try to learn to be patient, for in the early stages of your life and your career, financial benefit and promotion are likely to come slowly.

Your family is probably not wealthy and is unlikely to offer you financial help. Your powers of persistence should bring their own

Ox Outside the Gate

rewards, however. In the same way, your good behavior should help you to earn the respect of people in authority, and this is likely to be highly beneficial for your career.

RELATIONSHIPS
All Oxen Outside the Gate are likely to have their serious emotional relationships later in life. When you

have found the right partner, your relationship should be good, but try not to have children too quickly. Children may place unnecessary strain upon you when you are young. They will invariably force financial demands upon you, and you will be better equipped to face these challenges once you have begun to progress in your career.

YOUR CHINESE MONTH OF BIRTH

Find the table with your year of birth, and see where your birthday falls. For example, if you were born on August 30, 1949, you were born in Chinese month 7.

1 You are hardworking and successful, but can often appear to be awkward and distant.

2 You are happy and contented, but can occasionally be naive in your assessments of other people.

3 You are single-minded and prefer to be alone. You loathe criticism, but should try to listen.

4 You are determined to succeed and will make many sacrifices. Try to develop your compassion.

5 You are tough and hate to lose. You are also kind, however, and are always willing to join in.

6 You are outwardly confident, but inwardly worried. Learn to live with these personal contradictions.

7 Beware of your tendency to use any means to succeed. Try to listen more and to act less.

8 You are vivacious, likable, and attractive. Your strong personality should help you succeed in life.

9 You are compassionate, kind, and intelligent. Others like and trust you, but you should always beware of unscrupulous people.

10 You are successful and sociable. Your love life may start unhappily, but should eventually blossom.

11 You love to face a challenge and are a natural leader. You have a keen sense of justice, which can make you feel combative.

12 You are funny, determined, and a good friend. You might set yourself standards that are too high.

* Some Chinese years contain double months:	
1925: Month 4	1949: Month 7
April 23 – May 21	July 26 – Aug 23
May 22 – June 20	Aug 24 – Sept 21

1901			1913			1925	
Feb 19 – March 19	1		Feb 6 – March 7	1		Jan 24 – Feb 22	1
March 20 – April 18	2		March 8 – April 6	2		Feb 23 – March 23	2
April 19 – May 17	3		April 7 – May 5	3		March 24 – April 22	3
May 18 – June 15	4		May 6 – June 4	4		*See double months box*	4
June 16 – July 15	5		June 5 – July 3	5		June 21 – July 20	5
July 16 – Aug 13	6		July 4 – Aug 1	6		July 21 – Aug 18	6
Aug 14 – Sept 12	7		Aug 2 – Aug 31	7		Aug 19 – Sept 17	7
Sept 13 – Oct 11	8		Sept 1 – Sept 29	8		Sept 18 – Oct 17	8
Oct 12 – Nov 10	9		Sept 30 – Oct 28	9		Oct 18 – Nov 15	9
Nov 11 – Dec 10	10		Oct 29 – Nov 27	10		Nov 16 – Dec 15	10
Dec 11 – Jan 9 1902	11		Nov 28 – Dec 26	11		Dec 16 – Jan 13 1926	11
Jan 10 – Feb 7	12		Dec 27 – Jan 25 1914	12		Jan 14 – Feb 12	12

1937			1949			1961	
Feb 11 – March 12	1		Jan 29 – Feb 27	1		Feb 15 – March 16	1
March 13 – April 10	2		Feb 28 – March 28	2		March 17 – April 14	2
April 11 – May 9	3		March 29 – April 27	3		April 15 – May 14	3
May 10 – June 8	4		April 28 – May 27	4		May 15 – June 12	4
June 9 – July 7	5		May 28 – June 25	5		June 13 – July 12	5
July 8 – Aug 5	6		June 26 – July 25	6		July 13 – Aug 10	6
Aug 6 – Sept 4	7		*See double months box*	7		Aug 11 – Sept 9	7
Sept 5 – Oct 3	8		Sept 22 – Oct 21	8		Sept 10 – Oct 9	8
Oct 4 – Nov 2	9		Oct 22 – Nov 19	9		Oct 10 – Nov 7	9
Nov 3 – Dec 2	10		Nov 20 – Dec 19	10		Nov 8 – Dec 7	10
Dec 3 – Jan 1 1938	11		Dec 20 – Jan 17 1950	11		Dec 8 – Jan 5 1962	11
Jan 2 – Jan 30	12		Jan 18 – Feb 16	12		Jan 6 – Feb 4	12

1973			1985			1997	
Feb 3 – March 4	1		Feb 20 – March 20	1		Feb 7 – March 8	1
March 5 – April 2	2		March 21 – April 19	2		March 9 – April 6	2
April 3 – May 2	3		April 20 – May 19	3		April 7 – May 6	3
May 3 – May 31	4		May 20 – June 17	4		May 7 – June 4	4
June 1 – June 29	5		June 18 – July 17	5		June 5 – July 4	5
June 30 – July 29	6		July 18 – Aug 15	6		July 5 – Aug 2	6
July 30 – Aug 27	7		Aug 16 – Sept 14	7		Aug 3 – Sept 1	7
Aug 28 – Sept 25	8		Sept 15 – Oct 13	8		Sept 2 – Oct 1	8
Sept 26 – Oct 25	9		Oct 14 – Nov 11	9		Oct 2 – Oct 30	9
Oct 26 – Nov 24	10		Nov 12 – Dec 11	10		Oct 31 – Nov 29	10
Nov 25 – Dec 23	11		Dec 12 – Jan 9 1986	11		Nov 30 – Dec 29	11
Dec 24 – Jan 22 1974	12		Jan 10 – Feb 8	12		Dec 30 – Jan 27 1998	12

YOUR CHINESE
DAY OF BIRTH

Refer to the previous page to discover the beginning of your Chinese month of birth, then use the chart below to calculate your Chinese day of birth.

If you were born on May 5, 1901, your birthday is in the month starting on April 19. Find 19 on the chart below. Using 19 as the first day, count the days until you reach the date of your birthday. (Remember that not all months contain 31 days.) You were born on day 17 of the Chinese month.

If you were born in a Chinese double month, simply count the days from the first date of the month that contains your birthday.

1	2	3	4	5	6	7
8	9	10	11	12	13	14
15	16	17	18	19	20	21
22	23	24	25	26	27	28
29	30	31				

DAY 1, 10, 19, OR 28
You are trustworthy and set high standards, but tend to rush your

projects. Try to be cautious, and do not be too self-obsessed. You may receive unexpected money but must control your spending. You are suited to a career in the public sector or the arts.

DAY 2, 11, 20, OR 29
You are honest and popular. You need peace, but also require lively company. You are prone to outbursts of temper. You tend to enjoy life and make the most of your opportunities. You are suited to a literary or artistic career.

DAY 3, 12, 21, OR 30
You are quick-witted, but may appear to be difficult. As a result, people may be wary of being your friend. You have a disciplined character and fight for the truth. You are suited to careers that have a competitive element.

Day 4, 13, 22, or 31

You are very warmhearted, but also have a reserved attitude, which can sometimes make you appear unapproachable. If you try to be more outgoing and sociable, you should become more popular. You have a calm and patient manner, and are suited to a career as an academic or researcher.

Day 5, 14, or 23

Your fiery, obstinate nature can sometimes make it difficult for you to accept suggestions or opinions from others, and your stubbornness may lead to quarrels or problems. You should be lucky with money and may often use your profits to set up new projects. Your innate intelligence will enable you to cope with a demanding career.

Day 6, 15, or 24

You have an open, stable, and cheerful character, and enjoy an active social life. You are affectionate and emotional, and have a tendency to daydream. This can lead to confusion, and your eagerness to help others may be stifled by your indecision. Although you will never be wealthy, you should always have enough money.

Day 7, 16, or 25

You enjoy a certain amount of excitement in your life, but must learn to become more realistic and disciplined. Although you are a natural performer, you should beware of alienating your friends or colleagues. In your career, the opportunity to travel is more important to you than a good salary or a high standard of living.

Day 8, 17, or 26

You have very good judgment, but should not act too quickly. Your social skills may sometimes be lacking, and you may alienate other people, so try to be more tactful. You will experience poverty, but also wealth. Your calm and determined nature is combined with a free spirit, making you best suited to self-employment.

Day 9, 18, or 27

You are happy, optimistic, and warmhearted. You keep yourself busy and are rarely troubled by trivialities. Occasionally you quarrel unnecessarily with your friends, and it is important for you to learn to control your moods. You are particularly suited to a career as a sole owner or proprietor.

YOUR CHINESE
HOUR OF BIRTH

In Chinese time, one hour is equal to two Western hours.
Each Chinese double hour is associated with one of the
twelve astrological animals.

11 P.M. – 1 A.M. RAT HOUR
You are independent and have a hot temper. Try to think before you speak. Your thrifty nature will be useful in business and at home. You are willing to help those who are close to you, and they will return your support.

1 – 3 A.M. OX HOUR
Up to the age of twenty, your life could be difficult, but your fortunes are likely to improve after these troublesome years. In your career, be prepared to take a risk or to leave home during your youth to achieve your goals. You should enjoy a prosperous old age.

3 – 5 A.M. TIGER HOUR
You have a lively and creative nature, which may cause family arguments in your youth. Between the ages of twenty and forty you may

have many problems. Luckily, your fortunes are likely to improve dramatically in your forties.

5 – 7 A.M. RABBIT HOUR
Your parents should be helpful, but your siblings may be your rivals. You may have to move away from home to achieve your full potential at work. Your committed relationship may take time to become settled, but you should get along much better with everyone after middle age.

7 – 9 A.M. DRAGON HOUR
You have a quick-witted, determined, and attractive nature. Your life will be busy, but you could sometimes be lonely. You should achieve a good standard of living. Try to curb your excessive self-confidence, for it could make working relationships difficult.

9 – 11 A.M. SNAKE HOUR

You have a talent for business and should find it easy to build your career and provide for your family. You have a very generous spirit and will gladly help your friends when they are in trouble. Unfortunately, family relationships are unlikely to run smoothly.

11 A.M. – 1 P.M. HORSE HOUR

You are active, clever, and obstinate. Try to listen to advice. You are fascinated with travel and with changing your life. Learn to control your extravagance, for it could lead to financial suffering.

1 – 3 P.M. RAM HOUR

Steady relationships with your family, friends, or partners are difficult, because you have an active nature. You are clever, but must not force your views on others. Your fortunes will be at their lowest in your middle age.

3 – 5 P.M. MONKEY HOUR

You earn and spend money easily. Your character is attractive, but frustrating, too. Sometimes your parents are not able to give you adequate moral support. Your committed relationship should be good, but do not brood over emotional problems for too long – if you do your career could suffer.

5 – 7 P.M. ROOSTER HOUR

In your teenage years you may have many arguments with your family. There could even be a family division, which should eventually be resolved. You are trustworthy, kind, and warmhearted, and never intend to hurt other people.

7 – 9 P.M. DOG HOUR

Your brave, capable, hard-working nature is ideally suited to self-employment, and the forecast for your career is excellent. Try to control your impatience and vanity. The quality of your life is far more important to you than the amount of money you have saved.

9 – 11 P.M. PIG HOUR

You are particularly skilled at manual work and always set yourself high standards. Although you are warmhearted, you do not like to surround yourself with too many friends. However, the people who are close to you have your complete trust. You can be easily upset by others, but are able to forgive and forget quickly.

YOUR FORTUNE IN OTHER ANIMAL YEARS

The Ox's fortunes fluctuate during the twelve animal years. It is best to concentrate on a year's positive aspects, and to take care when faced with the seemingly negative.

YEAR OF THE RAT
This is a year of mixed fortunes. You are likely to be prone to illness throughout the Year of the Rat. However, do not despair – not everything is doom and gloom. Somewhat surprisingly, your career should progress smoothly this year.

YEAR OF THE OX
It may seem unjust, but the Year of the Ox is not necessarily a good year for an Ox. Your business, or your career, is likely to come under considerable threat, and areas in which you thought you might succeed and prosper could prove disappointing.

YEAR OF THE TIGER
Your family life is particularly auspicious during the Year of the Tiger, and marriage and children feature highly. Try to ensure that you spend enough quality time with your family during this excellent year.

YEAR OF THE RABBIT
Unfortunately, the Year of the Rabbit is an extremely inauspicious year for the Ox. Nothing will go smoothly – you are likely to experience many difficulties in various areas of your life, and illness and even death will seem to stalk your distant relatives.

YEAR OF THE DRAGON
Although the Year of the Dragon is a year in which you are likely to feel engulfed by troubles and problems, do not give in to feelings of despair. As long as you manage to keep yourself calm, you should find that everything can eventually be resolved.

YEAR OF THE SNAKE

Your fortunes are mixed in the Year of the Snake. For some of the time you will be successful, and money will be abundant. Suddenly, however, you will have to struggle against bad decisions and will find yourself entangled in various disagreements.

YEAR OF THE HORSE

This is a year in which you are well advised to stay calm, keep your own counsel, and bide your time. Try not to rush yourself in any areas of your life. Instead, be content to wait patiently for the benefits that time will inevitably bring.

YEAR OF THE RAM

Try to protect yourself, and beware of people who would like to take advantage of you or even cheat you. It is important not to let your guard slip, because in the Year of the Ram you are susceptible to people who might want to disrupt your life.

YEAR OF THE MONKEY

Success and good fortune follow you doggedly in the Year of the Monkey – everything that you decide to try your hand at works out astonishingly well. You will enjoy this year most if you celebrate this seemingly never-ending success with your family.

YEAR OF THE ROOSTER

It may seem unfair, but for no apparent reason, many of your friends could turn against you. Consequently, you are likely to find the Year of the Rooster very difficult, and your career is also likely to suffer as a result.

YEAR OF THE DOG

This is an interesting year. It is likely to be a time of travel, but also of loneliness. There will be many significant changes in your life, and some trouble, too, but the Year of the Dog should also be a time of considerable opportunity.

YEAR OF THE PIG

It is important for you to exercise care and restraint during the Year of the Pig. Your finances are likely to be overstretched, and as a result, you may find yourself having many serious quarrels and disagreements with members of your family.

YOUR CHINESE
YEAR OF BIRTH

Your astrological animal corresponds to the Chinese year of your birth. It is the single most important key in the quest to unlock your Chinese horoscope.

Find your Western year of birth in the left-hand column of the chart. Your Chinese astrological animal is on the same line as your year of birth in the right-hand column of the chart. If you were born in the beginning of the year, check the

middle column of the chart carefully. For example, if you were born in 1962, you might assume that you belong to the Year of the Tiger. However, if your birthday falls before February 5, you actually belong to the Year of the Ox.

1900	Jan 31 – Feb 18, 1901	Rat
1901	Feb 19 – Feb 7, 1902	Ox
1902	Feb 8 – Jan 28, 1903	Tiger
1903	Jan 29 – Feb 15, 1904	Rabbit
1904	Feb 16 – Feb 3, 1905	Dragon
1905	Feb 4 – Jan 24, 1906	Snake
1906	Jan 25 – Feb 12, 1907	Horse
1907	Feb 13 – Feb 1, 1908	Ram
1908	Feb 2 – Jan 21, 1909	Monkey
1909	Jan 22 – Feb 9, 1910	Rooster
1910	Feb 10 – Jan 29, 1911	Dog
1911	Jan 30 – Feb 17, 1912	Pig
1912	Feb 18 – Feb 5, 1913	Rat
1913	Feb 6 – Jan 25, 1914	Ox
1914	Jan 26 – Feb 13, 1915	Tiger
1915	Feb 14 – Feb 2, 1916	Rabbit
1916	Feb 3 – Jan 22, 1917	Dragon

1917	Jan 23 – Feb 10, 1918	Snake
1918	Feb 11 – Jan 31, 1919	Horse
1919	Feb 1 – Feb 19, 1920	Ram
1920	Feb 20 – Feb 7, 1921	Monkey
1921	Feb 8 – Jan 27, 1922	Rooster
1922	Jan 28 – Feb 15, 1923	Dog
1923	Feb 16 – Feb 4, 1924	Pig
1924	Feb 5 – Jan 23, 1925	Rat
1925	Jan 24 – Feb 12, 1926	Ox
1926	Feb 13 – Feb 1, 1927	Tiger
1927	Feb 2 – Jan 22, 1928	Rabbit
1928	Jan 23 – Feb 9, 1929	Dragon
1929	Feb 10 – Jan 29, 1930	Snake
1930	Jan 30 – Feb 16, 1931	Horse
1931	Feb 17 – Feb 5, 1932	Ram
1932	Feb 6 – Jan 25, 1933	Monkey
1933	Jan 26 – Feb 13, 1934	Rooster

1934	Feb 14 – Feb 3, 1935	Dog	1971	Jan 27 – Feb 14, 1972	Pig
1935	Feb 4 – Jan 23, 1936	Pig	1972	Feb 15 – Feb 2, 1973	Rat
1936	Jan 24 – Feb 10, 1937	Rat	1973	Feb 3 – Jan 22, 1974	Ox
1937	Feb 11 – Jan 30, 1938	Ox	1974	Jan 23 – Feb 10, 1975	Tiger
1938	Jan 31 – Feb 18, 1939	Tiger	1975	Feb 11 – Jan 30, 1976	Rabbit
1939	Feb 19 – Feb 7, 1940	Rabbit	1976	Jan 31 – Feb 17, 1977	Dragon
1940	Feb 8 – Jan 26, 1941	Dragon	1977	Feb 18 – Feb 6, 1978	Snake
1941	Jan 27 – Feb 14, 1942	Snake	1978	Feb 7 – Jan 27, 1979	Horse
1942	Feb 15 – Feb 4, 1943	Horse	1979	Jan 28 – Feb 15, 1980	Ram
1943	Feb 5 – Jan 24, 1944	Ram	1980	Feb 16 – Feb 4, 1981	Monkey
1944	Jan 25 – Feb 12, 1945	Monkey	1981	Feb 5 – Jan 24, 1982	Rooster
1945	Feb 13 – Feb 1, 1946	Rooster	1982	Jan 25 – Feb 12, 1983	Dog
1946	Feb 2 – Jan 21, 1947	Dog	1983	Feb 13 – Feb 1, 1984	Pig
1947	Jan 22 – Feb 9, 1948	Pig	1984	Feb 2 – Feb 19, 1985	Rat
1948	Feb 10 – Jan 28, 1949	Rat	1985	Feb 20 – Feb 8, 1986	Ox
1949	Jan 29 – Feb 16, 1950	Ox	1986	Feb 9 – Jan 28, 1987	Tiger
1950	Feb 17 – Feb 5, 1951	Tiger	1987	Jan 29 – Feb 16, 1988	Rabbit
1951	Feb 6 – Jan 26, 1952	Rabbit	1988	Feb 17 – Feb 5, 1989	Dragon
1952	Jan 27 – Feb 13, 1953	Dragon	1989	Feb 6 – Jan 26, 1990	Snake
1953	Feb 14 – Feb 2, 1954	Snake	1990	Jan 27 – Feb 14, 1991	Horse
1954	Feb 3 – Jan 23, 1955	Horse	1991	Feb 15 – Feb 3, 1992	Ram
1955	Jan 24 – Feb 11, 1956	Ram	1992	Feb 4 – Jan 22, 1993	Monkey
1956	Feb 12 – Jan 30, 1957	Monkey	1993	Jan 23 – Feb 9, 1994	Rooster
1957	Jan 31 – Feb 17, 1958	Rooster	1994	Feb 10 – Jan 30, 1995	Dog
1958	Feb 18 – Feb 7, 1959	Dog	1995	Jan 31 – Feb 18, 1996	Pig
1959	Feb 8 – Jan 27, 1960	Pig	1996	Feb 19 – Feb 6, 1997	Rat
1960	Jan 28 – Feb 14, 1961	Rat	1997	Feb 7 – Jan 27, 1998	Ox
1961	Feb 15 – Feb 4, 1962	Ox	1998	Jan 28 – Feb 15, 1999	Tiger
1962	Feb 5 – Jan 24, 1963	Tiger	1999	Feb 16 – Feb 4, 2000	Rabbit
1963	Jan 25 – Feb 12, 1964	Rabbit	2000	Feb 5 – Jan 23, 2001	Dragon
1964	Feb 13 – Feb 1, 1965	Dragon	2001	Jan 24 – Feb 11, 2002	Snake
1965	Feb 2 – Jan 20, 1966	Snake	2002	Feb 12 – Jan 31, 2003	Horse
1966	Jan 21 – Feb 8, 1967	Horse	2003	Feb 1 – Jan 21, 2004	Ram
1967	Feb 9 – Jan 29, 1968	Ram	2004	Jan 22 – Feb 8, 2005	Monkey
1968	Jan 30 – Feb 16, 1969	Monkey	2005	Feb 9 – Jan 28, 2006	Rooster
1969	Feb 17 – Feb 5, 1970	Rooster	2006	Jan 29 – Feb 17, 2007	Dog
1970	Feb 6 – Jan 26, 1971	Dog	2007	Feb 18 – Feb 6, 2008	Pig